Better Late Than Never

Stories of Me and She

Nansii Downer

HOMETOWN COMMUNITY PRESS

Better Late Than Never

- Stories of Me and She

© 2011 by Nansii Downer

Published by HomeTown Community Press
www.HomeTownCommunityPress.com

All rights reserved. No part of this publication may be reproduced, stored in a retrieval system, or transmitted in any form or by any means electronic, mechanical, photocopying, recording or otherwise without prior permission in writing from the author, except for brief quotations.

Printed in the United States of America

ISBN: 13: 978-0615579900
ISBN: 10: 0615579906

Cover art: Jaymes Downer

www.NansiiDowner.com
Twitter @NansiiD

Be sure to get Nansii's first book, 'The Redemption of Ruth'

This book is dedicated to my family and friends who have spent countless hours and years encouraging me to 'just write' and especially my dear friend, Claire De Ruvo who went the extra mile. For all the stories we have shared, the laughter, the tears this book is for you all. I know it has taken a while to get this book finished, but 'Better Late Than Never'! And yes, we have only just begun.

Introduction

This book is a collection of wacky stories of life. My life. The things that I do, or that happen around me, on a daily basis. Oh, they may seem pretty funny to you, alright. But for me, well they just seem kind of normal.

After all, doesn't everyone's husband practically set himself on fire when he is trying to light the fireplace? And don't you all battle a silent, hideous horror that lives in your plumbing? Just normal stuff, right?

Featured prominently on the cover of this book is my nemesis. My *She*. I dedicate this book to her only because, well, if it wasn't for her little voice encouraging me to get my BMI (body mass index) in order, I probably wouldn't be where I am today!

It was in the retelling of one of these crazy stories that one of my friends said "WOW girl, you need to write this stuff down!!" And the next thing I knew my husband had designed a blog for me. To be honest with you, I didn't even know what a blog was. But it was there, in cyberspace that I would document the humor known to my friends as "Nansii-isms". Things that they would shake they heads over and laugh out loud about and then write me back and say "Oh yeah, me too, girlfriend".

This book is filled with some of those stories. "Some" is the operative word here. Once I got started, well, it seemed like there would be no real end in sight. After all, funny just seems to follow me wherever I go. I hope that your day is brightened a little by something that you read. May GOD bless you!

Contents

1.	The Inspiration of Me and *She*	7
2.	A Little 'White' (and black) Lie	13
3.	H₂O Oh-Oh	19
4.	The Thrill of Victory	23
5.	Shrinking Pockets	27
6.	Texas Tried and True	29
7.	C for Me	33
8.	They're Baaaaaaack!!!	37
9.	Minding the P's and Q's	41
10.	The Season's Greeting	45
11.	Say Cheese!!	49
12.	Twas the Weak Before Christmas	53
13.	The Blizzard of Aught Nine	57
14.	Red Red Whine	61
15.	Getting Jiggly with My Bad Self	67
16.	Slip Slidin' Away	71
17.	Beware the Eyes of March	75
18.	Spring is in the Air	81
19.	Hair Today, Gone Tomorrow	85
20.	Does This Suit Suit Me?	91
21.	What Goes Around Goes to Round	95
22.	The Hunched Back of the Noted Dame	99
23.	Come On Baby Light My Fire	103
24.	Cutting Off My Knows to Spite My Face	107
25.	The Shedding	111
26.	The Heat is On	115
27.	Whistle Stop	119
28.	A Little Dab Will Do Ya	123
29.	Bad Moon Rising	127

Chapter 1

The Inspiration of Me and *She*

A few years ago my grandson Kodie received a great entertainment system for Christmas. I am not a big video game player at all. But I must confess, when my husband and I made our way upstairs to the game room and sat and watched him box I got really curious. It seemed like the character on the TV screen was moving right along with him. If he punched with his left hand so did the character. Quite different than the old video games that I remembered. Then he showed us the baseball and tennis games. Then he brought out the big guns.

Bowling.
 Oh my gosh!!!!

Talk about a kick in the pants. I was hooked. So hooked that we ended up bowling so long that we were actually sore the next day.

This past Christmas, my husband and son surprised me with the same entertainment system. I couldn't believe it. We immediately set it up and designed our characters and started bowling. I gotta tell you, my little alter ego is so cute. *She* looks just like me. Green eye shadow and a fancy purple outfit. *She* even has glasses. My son Jaymes' character wears one of those silly stocking cap things. Then there is my goofy husband who dresses his character in dark shades for that "extra" cool in-control look. We have even designed characters for our friends that come to visit and play with us. All three of us are Pro bowlers now, at least at home when we play.

In February I was surprised again with the fitness program add-on for the system. Now I must admit, I was quite happy with my bowling *She* and wasn't quite sure about the idea of exercising with a TV. Now if you know anything about these things, your character in the sports package is most likely going to look different from your character in the fitness area. To put it quite plainly... my little *She* character reflects my true body style.
Did you get that?
Yes indeed it is true.
This new character has the audacity of actually having this little tubby body that very much resembles mine. What happened to that bowling babe?????

Apparently when you type in the physical attributes that you possess the darn thing takes it seriously and makes the character in the "shape" of your real person. Drat the luck I say. But, I put a smile on my face and proceeded to sit back and prepare to laugh as Bryan and Jaymes built their characters. What the deuce???? Not an ounce of fat on either one of them. This might be a bit more difficult to bear than I had originally thought. It was OK if we were ALL going to look kinda pudgy, but just me????

That night we decided to do our first "Fitness Test." How many of you have a system like this? Isn't that the cutest little voice you have ever heard?

> It is so precious.
> Except during the body test.

My immediate mistake was going first. I should NEVER have done that. I remember stepping onto the board and it actually made a groaning sound. Have any of you heard that?

I mean, didn't you almost fall over? A groan????

It's a game for heaven's sake. The sound was almost personal. But before I could step off of the thing this cute little cartoon type voice says "That's OBESE!". I turned ever so slowly to get a look at my husband and son's faces. They were literally staring at the TV in disbelief. "Did that thing just say what I thought it said?" I demanded!

And then the unthinkable happened. They both started to laugh. Not just ha ha laugh, but the deep down belly laugh that makes your sides hurt. Then I got to laughing. Pretty soon we were all just busting up. I declared that very night that I would make her eat those words. No little three year old twit in a TV set was going to call me obese.

Now even though that moment *was* uncomfortable, it did indeed make me look at myself. I was overweight and out of shape but could this little scrap of a thing in a TV really help me get back on track? Well, I decided then and there that my little *She could* help me and we have been working out together ever since.
Well, not every day.
Old habits die hard ya know.

But I will tell you honestly, it was that little voice so politely telling me that I was obese that gave me the incentive to keep trying and by the end of May I had lost 20 pounds. Then the doldrums set in and I got lazy. That is the only way to explain it. Pure and simple lazy. I had almost given up until my husband took me to the movies.

We went and saw 'Julie and Julia' at the theater that weekend and the story of their story inspired me to finish what I had started. So I am back on my Fitness program. It really isn't that hard. It just takes a commitment and I really think I can do that. So I decided to write about it in case there are others who are lost and need to be found and put back on the right path.

Better Late Than Never – Nansii Downer

Together we can do it. We can share stories and motivate each other to keep going or try new moves. Or recipes. Or just a friendly chat. So join me on my journey, won't you? It will be fun and helpful to me to share my ups and downs, improvements and well you get the idea. I know that I have lots of friends out there that also work out . Join me when you can, OK?

My little *She* will make a better me!

Better Late Than Never – Nansii Downer

Chapter 2

A Little "White" (and black) Lie

Coming from a Catholic household I know the importance of differentiating between a white lie and the kind that are going to really warrant an hour long penance. I have always prided myself in a minimum of penance time. But every so often, a situation arises and I find I just can't control myself or the outcome. This was such a situation.

Chocolate sandwich cookies. Who among us doesn't just love them? I mean, come on now. Be honest. Do you eat them whole or are you a closet separatist? I carefully pull them apart and eat all of the naked ones first saving and savoring the delectable "middles" for last. Double filling is the best. My hands start to sweat just thinking about them. On occasion I enjoy them with a nice cold glass of milk. Other times, my thought is that the milk will just take up more cookie room.

I also enjoy reading a good novel. Murder mysteries are my favorite. Propped up in bed, leaning back against my fluffy pillows. **What could be better than that?** Why not have some cookies while I read? So I quietly went out to the kitchen and ever so slowly (so the bag wouldn't crinkle and make a bunch of noise) removed a handful of cookies and proceeded to quietly tip toe back to my room. Maybe this is where I should admit the problem started. You see, I had mentioned, just mentioned mind you, to my husband (who NEVER forgets anything I tell him) that I was going to start "watching my waistline".

I was going to eat better,
     exercise,
       walk the dog.

You know, all that stuff that you tell people to make yourself feel better. Anyway, I gingerly got back into bed with the paper towel (no crumbs in *this* bed, thank you very much) and got myself all set up to enjoy my book and my cookies.

  Carefully,
    Ever so carefully,
      I twisted those cookies apart,
    Separating the first eats
  From the last eats.

I laid them all out in a row, balanced on my tummy and then gently lifted the book and placed it right in front of the stack of cookies.

Now, I know what you are thinking. You think that I was trying to be sneaky, right? It wasn't exactly like that. I just really wanted some cookies and I didn't want my husband to feel pressured into reminding me that they probably weren't the best choice for a late night snack.

See.....I was thinking of *his* feelings. Wow, I can tell that one is going to cost me in penance.

Anyway... there I lay, propped up, book hiding, I mean shielding, no, no, no, disguising the fact that I had a napkin full of cookies, quite enjoying myself.

About the third naked cookie, I glanced up to see my husband standing at the foot of the bed. I gave him a very nice *closed mouth* smile. He smiles back at me. But then I notice that his line of vision has shifted to a different area, kind of above my head and to the right of me.

I mumble, "What's wrong Honey?" and he says, "I don't want to frighten you, but there is a lizard on the wall above the headboard".

Yeah right, I think. Lizard schmizard.

He must have looked at the dad-gum cookie bag and knows that I have cookies. About the same time as I was thinking this thought I turned my head ever so slightly and out of the reflection of my glasses I saw the outline of the

biggest lizard I had ever seen. Surely this **Iguana** must have escaped from the Fort Worth Zoo! **Faster** than I have personally ever moved in my entire life, I **flung** the covers off of me and literally **jumped** out of bed and ran out of my room. Here is where the complications set in.

You see, in my urgent quest to beat feet and get the heck out of that Komodo Dragon's way, **I forgot something very important.**

As I passed my husband like a speeding bullet, the cookies, *ALL* of those wonderfully perfectly separated "last eats" collided with my husband. I could hear him calling my name as the napkin gently floated down and landed at his feet. I silently went to get the vacuum. He remained where he was explaining to me what happens "when first we practice to deceive".

I have confessed this grievous sin to my *She*. It was shortly after this that she groaned when I proceeded to do my daily Fitness Test. Is it possible that she could groan louder?

I realized at that point that it was me and *She* against a world of cookies gone bad on my hips. I have vowed to look at the shadow I cast and work to create a smaller one. My wonderful *She* has promised to help me get to my goal.

Oh yeah. I almost forgot about the lizard. It was one of those tiny little gecko things and I am sure I heard him snickering at me as I carried him out to the front flower planter.

Better Late Than Never – Nansii Downer

Chapter 3

H2O Oh-Oh

Water. A precious commodity. The pitter patter of raindrops on a metal rooftop. The *chik-chik-chik* sound of a sprinkler in the late afternoon. The gentle whisper of the waves lapping the shoreline. Yes indeed. There is nothing quite like water.

That is, unless you have to force yourself to drink it like I do. I know that when GOD created everything He looked around and said "This is good". But I have often asked myself, exactly *who* on His angelic staff bothered to actually taste this stuff before declaring it "good"? Didn't He have a tasting committee?

My *She* prods me on a daily basis to remember the importance of drinking water while we work out. Oh man. I hate the stuff. Why does it have to taste... you know... so much like *water*?????

My good friend Dawn drinks water likes she actually enjoys the stuff. Who is she trying to kid here? She brings a bottle of water everywhere she goes. So does my Mom. If we go on even the quickest of errands she will ask in the most pleasant of "Mom" type voices, "Would you like a bottle of water to take with you, Nansii?" I think to myself, "Why? Don't they have Dr. Pepper where we're going?" Dr. Pepper *has* to be good for you. It's made from fruit, right?

After a 30 minute workout, the bells and whistles go off within the entertainment system fitness program and the time bank dances around for joy at your accomplishment. As the confetti fades from view this little message appears about it being a good time to "take a break and drink some water".

I almost throw myself down on the floor begging for mercy. "Wasn't the workout enough", I scream? Now I have to drink water too.

Good night Agnes.
Will the abuse never end?

But... I saunter to the kitchen and pour myself a tall glass of water, hold my nose and choke it down.

As time as gone by, I have slowly comes to terms that my *She* really wants the best for me. My friends (and you know who you are) have gently placed their arms about my shoulders and sang the praises of the virtues of water.

"Your skin will look younger".
Ok... I like that.
"It will help flush out your system".
Oh, that candy bar will be gone?
"It has absolutely, positively NO calories".
Now that's what *I'm* talking about!!!

Bring it on, I say. Crack those ice cube trays. Fill up that 16 ounce glass to the top. I have even learned a trick. If you squeeze a lemon in it and dump a package of sweetener on it you will think that you're having lemonade. Mind over matter, baby!

Better Late Than Never – Nansii Downer

Chapter 4

The Thrill of Victory

I come from a competitive family. We don't just play a game, we play to win. Don't play spoons with us... we'll take your hand off! Once when my parents were here visiting for the weekend we decided to play spades. My son Jaymes trumped my dad's trick much to my dad's chagrin. They were on the same team you see, so it wasn't necessary. But my son was focused on his own win so taking the trick just seemed natural.

I feel the same way when I work out. The "New Record" is what I live for. You even get your little *She* character's picture beside the score to record it for all time. Row after row of little *She's* smiling at my great accomplishments. Ah, yes. The winner in me arises.

I am a routine orientated person so I pretty much begin my day the same way every day.

Make the coffee,
    drink the coffee,
        read the paper.

Better Late Than Never – Nansii Downer

You know, easy living. The first morning that I got up and realized that I had added an exercise routine to my wonderful "alone" time was a big deal. Remember, it was me that wanted that entertainment system in the first place, but did I *really* want to do something with it? Reluctantly, I turned on the system and that wonderful captivating music that I have grown to love started to play and my competitive self took over.

I started with ski jumping. Have you tried that one? You are precariously balanced on the top of a ski slope waiting...

waiting...
waiting… until just the right moment and then

"Whoosh" down you go.

Squatting into the downhill slope until at the last second you straighten your knees and boost yourself to a standing leaning position for a smooth landing.

Just like the Winter Olympics, right?

Wrong, wrong, wrong.

It took me forever to learn how to lean just right and straightened up at just the exact, precise moment so that I didn't end up at the bottom of the ramp in the biggest snowball I had ever seen. Try again. Cute little *She* poised on the downhill bar... wait for it, wait for it, GO!!!

Squat, squat, squat…
    and…
        explode upward and balance.....
  balance......
and…… snowball at the bottom again.

"At least *She* looks really cute in her ski outfit" my husband reminds me me from the couch. I *will* conquer this, I vow.

Each day, my routine was the same.

Make coffee, drink coffee, read paper & workout.

It wasn't so much like exercise because I really was enjoying it. Yet, at the same time, my competitive juices were flowing. I could, no I *would* get the hang of this thing.

"I am woman, hear me roar!" I thought the first time *She* actually landed on her skis upright. The crowd cheers for you and you wave back with a smile on your face. And then the score is forever logged in. Oh yeah!!!! High score. And the music plays. Workout life is good. It is very good!

Better Late Than Never – Nansii Downer

Chapter 5

Shrinking Pockets

As a mother, it seems like I have always carried things in my pockets for my children. You know what I'm talking about.

Crayons, bubble gum, marbles.

The normal stuff kids desperately NEED to save. And as a mother, you are entrusted to hold them, until such time as the kids remember them or they go to bed whichever comes first. At the end of the day, it always amazed me to look at my pocket collection.

When we first started our cleaning service I would stick all kinds of stuff in my pockets so that I wouldn't vacuum them up. Paper clips, those little twist ties from the bread loaves. Stuff. I always had stuff in my pockets.

It seems recently that my pockets don't carry things as comfortably as they used to. I am sure that if I did a little research I would discover that it was some woman-hating men sitting around sewing machines in a factory somewhere making the pockets smaller. I mean, come on. It surely wasn't a woman's idea to do the tiny top part of the pocket in the same material as the pants only to have this HUGE wedge of bright white cloth sticking out of it once you get the pants on. **Have you seen a side view of that?????** It's a conspiracy, I tell you.

A few weeks ago I absentmindedly dropped some change into my pocket. It became uncomfortable, but diehard that I am, I didn't reach in there and take it out.

No, no, no,

I just proceeded on with my day. As I was getting changed for bed that evening I noticed the most peculiar thing. George Washington's face was embedded onto my leg. A little ink and I could have had a tattoo. **Good night Agnes.** When did my pockets get this small?????

She and I are now doing pocket duty. We have determined that we will work a little harder to make my pockets a little easier to work with. We now are learning to box. We enjoy it and it gives our pocket area a good workout. I am still not sure if this is some kind of a wardrobe conspiracy, but for right now we will work with what we've got.

Chapter 6

Texas Tried and True

I have noticed that people are flocking to Texas. Could it be the fabulous weather? Could it be the hill-less landscape? Could it be the big hair? Nah!!!!

What about all the bling we wear? Or those snake skin boots the cowboys wear? Or that down home country music that plays in all of the local honky tonks. Nope. It is none of these. I have been here now for 16 years now, and after doing much research I have found the answer to why people move here and why people stay here. It's the deep fried food!!!!

Each year at the Texas State Fair there is a contest to see who will come up with the best and most creative culinary fare. People from far and wide come and stroll around the fair grounds sampling all of the goodies that these fine folks come up with. Thousands of people walking around in a *Homer Simpson* daze as they sample the different treats. I have never seen so many happy contented people in one area. Texans love their food and by gosh they love it done right. And that means "deep fried". Oh yeah!!!

Better Late Than Never – Nansii Downer

Back in California, we would go to Disneyland and the treat of the day would be a funnel cake. Can't you just smell it as you read this? After it was fried just right and placed on a paper plate, they would sprinkle, no pour, the powdered sugar all over it. We would take it and sit down on one of the benches and pull it apart and eat it while it was still so warm it almost burned your mouth. It had just the right amount of crunch to it, yet the grease made it moist. Your fingers would be covered in this ooey-gooey sugary mess. Those were the good old days.

I really thought that no one would be able to top that. There couldn't possibly be anything better on a cool autumn night than delectable funnel cake.

But I was a foreigner in the land of deep fryers.

I had no earthly idea how many different "things" could be deep fried to take them to the cutting edge of cuisine. I am in Texas now, and it became my quest to seek all that this beautiful state had to offer. I traveled through the cities and tasted the foods that Texans so love.

Fried catfish, Chicken Fried Steak.

They even have Chicken Fried Chicken for those opposed to red meat. Aren't we thoughtful? I even had to join OEA after we had been here for a few months. I am sure that you know someone who is a member as well.

Better Late Than Never – Nansii Downer

Okra Eaters Anonymous

I never had fried okra in California. I was *so* hooked on it. Every restaurant we went to had to be a buffet so that I could get fried okra and lots of it. It took months of therapy to finally kick the habit.

A couple of years ago, we went to the State Fair with some friends. NEVER go anywhere with friends who can eat like there is no tomorrow. It is sooooo bad for your waistline. We visited every vendor to investigate what their magical deep friers were putting out. The choices were unbelievable. **Deep fried Twinkies** (come on now), **deep fried cookie dough** (saints be praised) and the winner of the prize... **deep fried peanut butter and jelly sandwiches.**

Good night Agnes. They had me. It didn't even matter what kind of jelly they were using. A PB&J dipped in a sweet pancake batter and then gingerly dropped into the scalding hot grease and fried to a delicate yet crispy crunch?????? **Oh Puh-leeze.** What is there not to love about this state? If you are looking for a warm place to live, where the countryside is nice and level and the music makes you want to tap you toes... **have I got a town for you.**

Better Late Than Never – Nansii Downer

Chapter 7

C for Me

Coughs and colds. Sniffles and sneezes. It happens every year at this time in towns around the world. Seasonal allergies and simple colds. Feed a cold, starve a fever. Extra doses of vitamin C. Sometimes I feel like I should buy stock in a tissue company. Why has there never been a true remedy for these simple germs?

While it is true that most of us *cowboy up* and suffer through these seemingly endless days of hacking and coughing, there are those who actually heed the advice of mothers long ago who declared, **"Stay home and stay in bed!"** Why do we attempt to tough it out and go about our days in misery? Usually, I must point out, sharing not only the misery, but the ill-laden germs with others. Do we secretly wish for those around us to feel as crummy as we do?

And for heaven's sake, why does everyone in the office stop by MY desk with a drippy nose to get a tissue? What????? Am I the only one in the entire office that buys these handy sneeze catchers?

Better Late Than Never – Nansii Downer

Think about it. If everyone would stay home when they were sick, then the rest of us could muddle through and just get the job done. **But NO.** In you come to work, dragging your woebegone chin on the floor, looking to tell anyone that will listen how crummy you feel. The whole time that you are talking, you are spewing vile germs into my workspace.

Dontcha care about me at all???

But I have decided that you won't win. **No, no, no.** I am going to fight back. Germs and flu bugs be gone. What better way to feel good than to take some extra vitamin C and exercise more. My little *She* agrees. We can fight this and win, *She* said. It just takes a little common sense, and that, *She* has plenty of. Actually, I think it has helped. I haven't coughed or sneezed this whole season. And *She* no longer says the dreaded word, "OBESE" to me anymore. How great is that? Every time I see her, she has a smile on her face and a healthy glow to her skin.

I am not afraid to go out in public. Those bad germs won't get hold of me. **I am lookin' good and feelin' good.** Yes sir. We are on the move. A thinner, healthier me now occupies that office space. As a matter of fact, we may even go to the State Fair this year. I've got nothing to fear being in a crowd. Besides, I hear that the new food offerings go hand in hand with the season. Remember, we deep fry everything. This year it's butter. Who new that was even possible?

Well, never fear. If you are leery about being out where there are lots of sick folks breathing their germs all over you, you don't have to fear the State Fair.

This year's newest addition is **Deep Fried Hand Sanitizer**

Who knew?????

Better Late Than Never – Nansii Downer

Chapter 8

They're Baaaaaaack!!!

Oh my gosh, I can't believe it. The most wonderful thing has happened. All of you young mothers out there take heart. Your days of fussin' and fightin' with your children in the morning to get them dressed for school are over. Do you hear me? Jump for joy, because I saw the commercial. Garranimals are back.

In the early 70's (oh my goodness... some of you were just babes yourselves), the most wonderful idea was born in the clothing department. They were called Garranimals. Does anyone remember these life savers? Mornings no longer held the dreaded "this doesn't match". Garranimals were MADE to match. And they were such fun to match up. Each animal was color coordinated for easy matching. Monkeys went with monkeys, giraffes with giraffes. The animal kingdom reigned supreme in our house.

It was easy. It was fun. And face it... it was simple. No guess work. Look at the little picture on the tag on the collar of the shirt and then go to the closet and find the pair of pants that had the same animal. Anyone could dress their children for success. Ingenious I tell you.

Better Late Than Never – Nansii Downer

I have never been one to mix and match my colors or fabrics.

> Black shirt? Simple... black pants.
> Blue pants? Easy… a matching blue blouse.

If I was really feeling bold the red blouse might have a different accent color in it. But let's not get crazy. Green with green, blue with blue. You get the idea right? It was simple really. **A recipe for success.** Well, it was until recently.

As anyone who knows me well can attest, I love the color purple. My bowling ball and towel are purple. I have lots of shades of purple eyeshadow and scrunchies for my hair. Purple is for royalty. Purple is peaceful. Purple is the color that my *She* wears, except when she is working out.

Whose idea was it to put her in white? Have you seen what happens to us when we wear white? I try never to outdo her with my mad wardrobe skills so I got a white workout outfit too. I would put it on in the morning to do my yoga routine with her. I boldly wore it while performing my advanced step with her. I wore it proudly. Until I actually saw myself in the mirror. Something was wrong. I did not look cute like *She* did. White on white does not necessarily make cute on cute. I looked like a very bad version of a Pillsbury Dough boy. What was *She* thinking? *She* should have told me that we didn't look our best. It should have come from her BEFORE I got a full view of myself in the bedroom mirror. The gasp that escaped from me could be heard blocks away. The look of a wet marshmallow was not what I was going for.

So, I realize that the Garranimal look might not be for everyone. Oh you young mothers should still do yourself a favor and stock up on them. Save your stress for the things that really matter in life. What to make for dinner and how to get those precious little babies down for that much needed nap. For me, however, I am going to put on my blue jammie bottoms with my blue jammie top. You know… the ones with the cute little monkeys on it. Ah the bliss!

Better Late Than Never – Nansii Downer

Chapter 9

Minding the P's and Q's

One of the nice things about residing in Texas is that we actually experience seasonal weather changes. Being a native of California, this is quite a phenomenon. There is just something special about that first morning when I grab my cup of coffee and go outside and notice, with much awe and relief, that I am not dripping wet from the Texas heat. You gotta admit... we know heat. And I am not talking about a spicy Tex-Mex dish. I am talking about being able to fry an egg on the back porch by about 9 am throughout the summer. **Good night Agnes it gets hot here.**

But then... around the end of September, after all of those spring and summer storms have made their way through our town, a blessed relief comes. **We call it Fall.** Cooler temps and bluer skies. Afternoon iced tea is slowly replaced with the occasional cup of coffee. Instead of the grill being fired up every night, we actually turn the oven on again and bake a roast or a meatloaf. After all, if it's below 90 degrees Fall must be just a few weeks away.

Personally, I like the cold weather. I just can't peel enough clothes off in the summer without offending the neighbors. I hate sweating. It's just so... oh I don't know... eeky. With the cooler weather I can cover things up that shouldn't really be visible anyway. It just makes good sense. I follow the rule: "If you've got too much of it, for heaven's sake cover it up".

The only problem I have had of late with the weather cooling off is pantyhose. Why, oh why were these abominations created?
          To taunt me?
                To suffocate me?
                        To totally humiliate me????

Last winter, I decided to wear a skirt to the office. Sooooooo, I got into the *treasure drawer of undergarments* and dug out a new pair of pantyhose. Now they seemed a smidge hard to get into but I attributed that to still being "damp" from my shower.

This particular day I was up and down up and down multiple times. In the early afternoon I noticed that the back of my legs were tired and achy. I convinced myself it was because I had been up and down so much and I was just getting tired. Then I noticed that my legs were almost feeling numb. I must admit I got concerned. I kind of stretched a bit and sat up a bit straighter to relieve the pressure I was feeling and continued working. Finally, I couldn't stand the pain anymore and stood up and started to rub the top of my legs. It was then I discovered this huge lump on my rump.

What the heck?

I made my way to the ladies room and discovered (with much embarrassed laughter) that my pantyhose had decided they would roll down and they were cutting off my circulation!!!! I was stunned. Shocked. By gosh I was taking those pantyhose back because obviously they were flawed.

Just exactly what DO those letters stand for on the inside of the pantyhose?

I am a "P" I tell you. A "P"!

Why in the world would a company that I have faithfully bought pantyhose from for all of these years suddenly change the size dimensions without telling me? Is this some kind of a cruel joke?

What? What did you say? A "P" is only for women of smaller stature? As in height only? I am a "Q"????? Are you serious? The "Q" pantyhose were made with women like me in mind? The letter "Q" comes after the letter "P" for a reason? I should have been warned. Nothing like this should be sprung on a person. I needed time to prepare. A "Q," huh.

My *She* and I decided after that incident to try to get back to being a "P". Oh we know it will take some time and dedication. Hey, that "Q" didn't happen overnight. But, as a team we will change things. But for now? I am going to be the best "P" I can, inside the body of a "Q".

Chapter 10

The Season's Greeting

I must admit that the Christmas season is one of my favorite times of year. I love all of the lights, the music, and the cinnamon apple candles burning. It's just so… oh you know... Christmassy.

It just puts a smile on my face to hear Linus recite his Christmas story for the 100th time. Or to laugh over and over as Ralphy gets told "You'll shoot your eye out!" No matter how many times I play my "Holiday Classics" CD, I never tire of the melodies. Ahhh....there is just something about it all.

The day after Thanksgiving is the day we decorate the house. Or should I say, "I" decorate the house. My husband is in charge of the outside and I do the inside. He drags his big ol' ladder in and struggles to get it placed just right under the attic door. We have one of those funky ceiling doors that you tug on a rope and the door drops open and behold... boxes…

…and boxes
and boxes…

…did I tell you there were BOXES? I must say, I have been collecting Christmas decoration from around the world for years now. Well, maybe not around the world exactly, but from discount stores that are *out of my area* at least.

Snowmen too numerous to count!

But all so cute that I can't part with any of them. Big ones, small ones, some are on pillows, some are on throw blankets. Towels, plates, coffee cups. It's like Frosty himself has brought his entire family to reside at my house for the duration of the winter.

The entire weekend is spent with Christmas music playing and me "ho-ho-ho-ing" merrily along.

I remember in California, the weather never really got very cold, so the first few winters here in Texas were a shock to me. As a matter of fact, the first real cold snap is still a shock to me. Last week I was contemplating crop pants and this week I am looking to find the wool socks and warm jammies. The aroma of a big ol' pot of chili cooking brings my guys to the table. After all, we have all worked hard to get the house looking wonderful. The outside lights are finished and the tree is ready for its final addition of the candy canes. All is well in my holiday world.

That is… until the dreaded plastic tubs of winter clothing are placed within my sight. I am up to 4 of them now. Oh, trust me; it is *not* because I have so many cute holiday type sweaters. No, no, nooooo. It's because I have saved the different

SIZES of those adorable, sparkly, I know-I-will-eventually-be-able-to-wear-this-again-sweaters!!!!

It's like a sickness I tell you. I haven't been a size 4 since I don't know when, but this little voice in my head says, "You never know... wouldn't it just be a shame if you got rid of this oh-so-cute little sweater and next year you lost more weight than would be humanly possible and it mysteriously would have fit you?"

Can I get an amen here?????

I can't imagine that I am the only woman in the world who saves the improbable in hopes of accomplishing the near impossible. And then, to make myself feel even worse?????? I try them all on!!!! Oh the humility of it all.

Why in the world I venture to think that a year in a plastic tub is going to somehow change the dimensions of those sweaters and pants is absolutely beyond me. But each year it's the same thing…

..Year after year after year.

And then, exhausted, I lovingly fold them all up and place them gently back in their respective tubs to wait until the first chill the next year. Family traditions are so hard to break.

Better Late Than Never – Nansii Downer

Chapter 11

Say Cheese!!!

Saaaayyyy Cheese!!!! It's such a cute little way to make you smile for a photo op. Everyone says it. No matter where you travel in the world, when someone says those magic words everybody turns to the camera and displays their pearly whites. I bet you can't think of one professional photographer who doesn't pull this little verbiage out of his pocket when he is trying to get that "just so perfect" picture. Big smiles for all. I mean, after all, who doesn't like cheese?

As a young mother, I found that I could pretty much put a slice of this delectable stuff in any sandwich and my kids would scarf it down. Want them to eat their broccoli? Melt some cheese over the steaming hot vegetable and it is gone in seconds. Sprinkle some cheese from a jar and make your plain old spaghetti the hit of the night. Burgers, french fries, even salads have been adorned with this wonder of all wonders. Appetizers of fried cheese are on menus accompanied with marinara sauce for dipping. Toasted cheese sandwiches with a hot bowl of soup. Huge baked potatoes with melted cheese dripping down the sides with another favorite, butter. Ahh, the wonderful memories of it all.

Better Late Than Never – Nansii Downer

My mom always makes this awesomely wonderful Asparagus Casserole for Thanksgiving and Christmas. It is baked to a perfect done-ness and then at the last minute she takes the cover off and lets the cheese get this golden crispy brown. It is to die for. The recipe calls for the juice from the cans of asparagus being stirred and heated with a jar of processed cheese for the sauce. Then you dice up 1/2 a dozen hard boiled eggs and a bunch of saltine crackers smashed ever so fine and layer it all in a baking dish. Can't ya just *FEEL* your arteries clogging up as you read this???? I know now why it only gets made at the holidays. We would all be wearing pacemakers from the heart attacks if she made it more.

I sometimes ask myself, "When did the change happen to me"? You know. At what point did the "I can eat whatever I want and never put on a pound" change to "Oh my gosh... those pants are *WHAT* size?"

This shouldn't happen to anyone. How am I supposed to convince my children to eat their cheese-laden broccoli spears when I am forced to look them in the eye and tell them, "Well, I am watching my weight so I can't have cheese".

I mean, *Come On!!!!* As a mother it is my responsibility to teach by example, right? After all, when we decided to have children we made a commitment to them. To teach them, show them, and that's right, eat the same things that we want them to eat. It's my job. I should EAT the cheesy gooey yummy broccoli to show them how it is done. Right? Right? RIGHT?

These last few months, me and *She* have been paying attention to the little things. You know. The calories. Now I am not saying that I never eat cheese anymore. No, no, no. But I do try to eat it less often. It's kind of like a trade off. I don't consume too much cheese and my hips feel better in the morning. It's not really so bad.

With the children grown and living on their own now, the pressure to set a good example at the dinner table has been averted. We now add just a smidgen of seasoned salt to our veggies for that "oh so almost good" flavor. After all, we are adults. We don't need to cover up the wholesome natural flavor of our vegetables anymore, right? We can handle the taste of any ol' steamed vegetable and at least LOOK like we're enjoying it naked. What's that honey? The grand-kids are coming to spend the night with us? Wooo Hooo! Break out the extra cheese and buttered popcorn. I feel a good example coming on.

Better Late Than Never – Nansii Downer

Chapter 12

Twas the Weak Before Christmas

Twas the "weak" before Christmas.
And out on my porch
I was watching intently
For the "Ups" man of course.

The stockings were hung
On the old family hutch,
With no fireplace for us
This will work in a clutch.

With me in my apron
Just baking away,
The cookies and breads
For our big family day.

The presents were wrapped
With the ribbon and bows,
The music was playing
Ahh yes, it's my zone.

Then all of a sudden,
My dogs start to chatter.
I rose from my chair
To see what was the matter.

Better Late Than Never – Nansii Downer

I ran to the parlor,
Threw open the door.
I knew he was coming
And who the present was for.

Then what to my wandering eyes
Did I see?
That big old brown truck
He was parked by my tree.

I jumped off the porch
And I ran to his side
I signed my John Hancock
And my smile did not hide.

He might have worn brown
And his tummy didn't jiggle.
But I knew in my heart
He was really Kris Kringle.

I carefully carried
The box with such glee,
And put it down gently,
'Cause this one's for me!!

Better Late Than Never – Nansii Downer

I turned and I waved
And I bid him adieu
I knew in my heart,
He had plenty to do.

Yet I heard him exclaim
As he drove down my road.
"Merry Christmas to all,
I have finished my load!"

Better Late Than Never – Nansii Downer

Chapter 13

The Blizzard of Aught Nine

Oh yes. I was there. I will be able to tell my grandchildren all about the storm that took the town by surprise. Wichita Falls, Texas has indeed made a name for itself. You thought they got a lot of publicity when the Cowboys decided to train there? Well, that was nothing my friend. Nothing compared to the stories that will regale about the Blizzard of Aught Nine.

Bryan, Jaymes, the 2 dogs and I arrived by suppertime the night before Christmas Eve. We parked the car on the grass in the folk's backyard and unloaded our gift laden Toyota. Since other family members were joining us for the holiday, we readily agreed to sleep in the travel trailer parked in the yard in its custom made carport. It gives us plenty of room to move around and the privacy and quiet that we sometimes crave when there are lots of people around. Besides that, I prefer not *EVERY*-one see me in the morning. It's hard enough on my husband, son and dogs.

By nature, I think that's what the cause is, I am an early riser, usually, no later than around 5:30 a.m. I have the coffee going and am getting ready to let the dogs go out. This morning would be no different.

Better Late Than Never – Nansii Downer

At least where the time was concerned. When I opened the trailer door it was raining pretty hard. So I caught the dogs and we all agreed that we would wait awhile before stepping out to do our business. I crawled back into bed and snuggled down to catch a few more winks. After all, this was vacation right?

When my eyes opened again, I was shocked to see that I had slept in. **Me! Sleeping past 8????** "My goodness," I thought as I once again prepared to take the dogs out, "I must have really needed the extra rest". From the quiet, I could tell that the rain had finally let up so I went ahead and opened the door for the dogs. I now have a PRETTY good idea what the term **"The first step is a doosey"** means. It seems that while I was nestled all snug in my bed, old man winter had decided to drop a couple of inches of snow!!!!!!!

That first metal step out of the trailer dang near landed me in the hospital. As I drug myself back inside, I took one last look towards the house. The path was a slushy, icy mess. What were we going to do???? We only had enough good water for one pot of coffee and I could polish that off by myself. Our other staples consisted of the thawing turkey and the extra orange juice. All of the delicious cookies and candies and fudge that I made for this wonderful gathering, were inside the house with those other family members. **We were doomed.**

Better Late Than Never – Nansii Downer

So I did what any red blooded American would do in a crisis situation. I reached for my cell phone and called my mom, who was of course staying in the house with those other family members. She answers the phone in her most preciously calm yet chipper voice, "Good morning sweetheart. Did you sleep well?"

I am appalled.
"Did I sleep well????"

I choke out my reply. "Have ya even looked out your dad-gum back door and noticed that SOME of your family is snowed in, without food or water?" I so wanted to say, but didn't. "Mom, maybe you should open the sliding glass curtains and take a look outside", I coo instead. "Oh my" she says quietly, "When did it start to snow? Oh look kids... it's snowing... come and see... What did you say dear?"

Finally, after putting on every article of clothing that we brought, the three of us slip, slide and slush our way, what seems like a mile and a half, to the back door with our snowy wet dogs on our heels. And for the next 12 hours the snow keeps coming...
    and coming...
        and coming.

Would it never stop we cried. It was like there was a little energizer snowman huffing and puffing from the clouds.

Better Late Than Never – Nansii Downer

Our car was buried in the backyard. The carport over the trailer looked like it could collapse at anytime. Later that morning, my dad decided he should test the roads and go to the market. I was sitting in the recliner the whole time and I swear I didn't know that they were stuck in the street half in and half out of the driveway for over 30 minutes, until I heard the neighbor talking to them about giving them a push. Bryan says I need to pay more attention to things like that. I say, "Don't try to drive in the snow ".

When the blowing wind and snow finally stopped, we all sighed in relief. The crisis was over. We were all safe and sound and could now stop worrying. But then I thought back on our previous night. We had made popcorn and watched "The Christmas Story" and laughed like crazy. Together. We had spent Christmas morning eating a great breakfast, opening presents and preparing the turkey and all of the fixings. Together. We watched football, played cards and ate every smidgen of the fudge I brought. Together. I guess it doesn't really sound so bad after all does it? You know how we Texans are... we always have to have a great story to tell to the kids. And this will be mine.

Chapter 14

Red Red Whine

I have often wondered who makes the decisions about what we should and shouldn't wear. Haven't you? Is it some **high class diamond dripping vamp** sitting at her desk on the 50th floor of a downtown New York City office? Could it be the *'never a hair out of place'* **Donald** type **guy** who marries only the best dressed woman in the world? Is the cheesy looking guy that stops at the coffee house each morning and sits and pours over the latest magazines?????

Come on... aren't you the least bit curious to know who it is that sets these fashion trends in place? Well search no more. I have the answer and I am willing to share this timely secret with you. It's my Mom and her best friend.

They are without a doubt the *Fashionistas* of their town. The women in Wichita Falls would be running around stark naked if it wasn't for their keen eye to the latest fashion "Ins" and "Outs". It is amazing to watch them in action. The sales clerks tremble when they see them walk into their shops. These women are known around town I tell you. They can "make" or "break" a shop. I am sure that they must be inundated daily with emails and calls from around the world seeking their advice on fabric trends, skirt lengths and of course, color.

If you want to know what is hot and what is not, these two fine ladies are there for the asking. Even if you really don't want to hear the answer.

Winter is a special time for me. I enjoy the sights and sounds. The baking and gift wrapping. The holiday sweaters that just scream to be worn joyfully. As mom would always say, **"Red is such a bold wonderful color. Use it to your advantage. It commands respect."** Since a good dose of respect is something I always like my fellow man to give me, I set my sights, and heart on something new…

…something bold

…something that I have never owned before

…red pants.

Yep. I tell her that I am going to buy a pair of red jeans or red dress pants. It was a lovely day, both of us enjoying a fresh cup of her delicious coffee. Mother and daughter sharing quality time together at her dining room table, with Christmas music playing softly in the background. It just doesn't get much better than that.

Until I mentioned the red pants.

With every ounce of finesse she has, she gingerly sets her cup on the table, looks at me lovingly and says *"Really?"*

Better Late Than Never – Nansii Downer

I don't know about any of you but when my Mom says *"really"* like that, it usually means something more like "Have you totally lost your mind????!!!!"

I slowly set my cup down and wait. And wait. Eventually she will spill it. They always do. Even when you have given birth to their grandchildren, they will ALWAYS be Mom. Good sound, solid advice is never more than a phone call away, right? Just ask me. I am a mother too. I know how this works.

Ever so gently she clears her throat and begins, "Dear, there are certain things that women of our, (*cough cough*), size should not wear. One of those items is red pants. Trust me. You don't want to do this. Red should only be worn *above* the waist. When you are leaving a room, in red pants, you will look like a Christmas ornament…

…A very BIG Christmas ornament".

I blinked twice to cover my amazement. An ornament????? A *big* ornament at that. She *must* be wrong on this one. Her fashion sense must have had a momentary lapse. I wanted red pants... by gosh I HAD to have red pants. All of a sudden the thought of not having red pants was almost too much to bear. But, the good daughter that I am, I sighed and thanked her for her wonderful forethought on this issue and let the subject drop.

We arrived home on Sunday afternoon and the next day I had my husband promptly take me to the mall. I was going to show her alright. I was going to go to every store that was in that mall until I found them and owned them. Red pants. I was on a mission. The holidays were still upon us so they shouldn't be too hard to find. In my mind, every store in the mall should be stocked to the rafters with red pants. I would visit every store if that is what it took. Time stood still as we made our way around the mall.

Finally, we came to a shop that caters to petite sized women. Remember???? That's what I am... *petite.* So in I go, shoulders squared, head held high straight to the first sales lady I see. "Of course we have red pants", she assures me. We travel to the rack and what do my eyes behold but pair after pair of red pants. And believe it or not, all of the skinny girls had already been there and left plenty of "my" sizes. From 12 up to 18 there were dozens of them. It was a bounty. I grabbed a pair, told my husband to have a seat and dashed into the dressing room.

There is no way to express the bliss of knowing that in a few short minutes I was going to be floating out of the store with my new red pants. I pulled them on and twirled around to get a mirrored view. I pranced out of the room and practically danced in front of my husband anxiously waiting for him to tell me how great they looked.

But then I noticed it.
The raised eyebrow.
The one that speaks volumes without saying a word.

"Turn around" he whispered. I do so. And I wait... and wait. I turn back around and see that he is standing up ready to go. He says one word and one word only,

"Ornament"

I called my Mom a few days later and in passing mentioned my little shopping excursion. I could see her smiling though the phone, but she never uttered the words "I told you so". She didn't have to. After all, I'm a Mom too. I just *shoulda* known.

Better Late Than Never – Nansii Downer

Chapter 15

Getting Jiggly with my Bad Self

This past year I incorporated working out with my morning routine. Let's be very clear here, though. My morning routine would not likely have been considered healthy by most. After several cups of coffee, you know, the strong, put hair on your chest stuff, my exercise consisted of opening the back door to let my dogs out. If I was really feeling energetic, I might even stroll out onto the back porch and gently toss the ball around for my dogs. So when I got this wild idea that a little exercise might do me some good, it was a real ground shaker in my house. It's not like they doubted that I would do it, but hey, they know me. Sitting quietly is more my speed.

I must admit, it took quite a bit of time to create poetry in motion but I do believe that I have a handle on it now.
My *She* and I can change it up with the best of them.

Kick Boxing? Yeah, we do it.
Yoga? Oh my, look at that perfect posture.
Step Dance? We could be on "So You Think You Can Dance".

We are good, I tell ya. **Dang good.** Once that music starts playing we are one with it. That balance board has nothing on us. Floating like a butterfly. Yep, that's us. I was feeling so confident that I decided to add a little spice to the workout. You know, keep it fresh, keep it alive. I was an old hand at this now. There was nothing I couldn't do.

Until I decided to try the Hula Hoops. Who's idea was it to put *that* in the program. This was supposed to be a fun way to get in shape. What's a little sweat between friends, right? This should have been an easy thing for my *She* and I. But NOOOOOO!!!! I am saddened and ashamed to report that we are sorely missing the mark in this little exercise of wit. And it is all my *She*'s fault. She has no rhythm.

Once the music starts you twirl your hips while keeping the Hula Hoop spinning. Oh it sounds easy enough, doesn't it. Once you get them babies twirling some other character in the corner of the screen (and I think I know who it is) tosses another hoop to you. Now you must catch it while still twirling the other hoop. Not bad? Try another... and another.

The tossers never miss a beat while I frantically try and remember which way to twirl so I don't lose any points. I *AM* **all about winning** you know. This is usually about the time that I am making some incredible growling type sounds so both dogs come in the room to see what is happening and start to bark at me, thinking that I must be growling at the bad guy.

Better Late Than Never – Nansii Downer

Next comes my husband. He just stands there staring. What can he say after all? I am frantically twirling invisible hoops and cursing under my breath, blaming the DNA that my father must have passed to me that is causing me to have to exercise in the first place. I have sweat running down my cheeks and my *She* looks fresh as a daisy. Is there no justice? This just doesn't seem fair.

We all know that I am all about what's *fair,* so after I caught my breath from the invigorating workout, I grabbed another cup of coffee, sat down at the table, and thought about how I might even things up a bit.

She doesn't sweat.

She never even looks ruffled after a 30 minute workout.

She eats what *She* wants when *She* wants and only changes weight when I do. Huh. Something is just not right here. I leer at her over the lip of my coffee cup.

Thinking, thinking. I've got it!!!!

I'll show her a thing or two. I will beat her at her own game.

I must have had a real scary look on my face because my husband walked by and stopped and just kind of looked at me. And then he quietly walked away shaking his head wondering what in the world I could be up to. I rose from the table and walked back to the controller. I knew what I had to do. It just was not working having her look better than me. So I took off her eye makeup.

That showed her a thing or two!

Chapter 16

Slip Slidin' Away

I have recently discovered that the rules of "I just have to have that" do not just apply to those precious little knee huggers at Christmastime. Oh no. There seem to be plenty of folks over the age of "You should know better than to believe that crud" living around me. Some of them even live at my house. Imagine that.

I would venture to say with the utmost of certainty that most of us seek a good night's sleep. I know I do. My husband is a tosser and turner. You know the kind. By the end of the day his back is sore and something about laying still for several hours doesn't work well. It takes him about a minute to fall into this deep, deep sleep then he spends the next several hours tossing and turning. He just never seems to get comfortable.

Back and forth…
 …back and forth.
Grab the pillow…
 …fluff the pillow.

Sheet tucked in and sheet tucked out. Even the dogs leave the room to go and find a quiet place to get some rest. It's amazing that I look as good as I do in the morning!!!

Better Late Than Never – Nansii Downer

On a recent trip to the local membership store, he spotted a huge display of the "World's Best Pillows".

"Maybe a new pillow would help," he said as he picked one up. These things weighed about 5 pounds and were so thick you could leave a hand print in them that took several minutes to go away. "Wow" I said. "Once you lay your head down on that thing you will never move again". Not a bad idea I thought to myself. Maybe this will eliminate the night spasms and we will both look great in the morning.

Now, these things weren't cheap so we decided to buy just one and we would both test it out and see what we thought. I must admit that first night I was a bit green with pillow envy as he lay ever so quietly breathing in and breathing out with a slight smile on his face. Blissful rest. I just gotta have one of those pillows too.

Then I saw it! Sitting in my own living room watching a Saturday afternoon rerun. The thing that promised *me* a good night's sleep. A mattress pad made out of the very same miracle material that my husband's pillow was made out of. Oh my gosh! I was so excited I almost forgot to breathe. And the commercial for it was so informative and believable. "A simple mattress pad that would guarantee the best night's sleep humanly possible". Morning stiffness and back aches would be a thing of the past. You are cradled to sleep and your body is tenderly wrapped in the firmness of the most incredible mattress pad a person could ever ask for. **Brilliant, just brilliant.** Whoever discovered this patent had my vote for person of the year. According to the commercial, and we all *know* there is only truth in commercials, you could even jump up and down on your side of the bed in your skimpy negligee while your mate has a glass of wine balanced precariously beside his toes. Wow. I was sold. We were getting one of those…

…And we did.

Now, I am not one to complain, but there is something amiss with my new mattress pad. Oh it is firm enough, just like the advertisement said. You can press on it and your handprint will remain for several minutes. But it is having a smidgen of a problem staying "in place" on our pillowtop mattress. Remember those???? Oh don't date me now, but yes, we still have a pillowtop mattress. It's only about 1/8 of an inch thick but that is just enough to throw the new mattress pad off kilter.

I first noticed that I would wake up in the morning gripping the side of the bed with the most peculiar feeling that I was falling off a cliff. It has come to my attention that the mattress pad shifts to the right every night causing a couple of inches to hang off my side of the bed. I found this out one morning as I sat down and reached into my closet for my shoes.

Better Late Than Never – Nansii Downer

I slid off the bed and into the closet in a split second. This was *NOT* mentioned in the commercial. I was devastated. Can you imagine my turmoil? What was I to do? Get rid of it?

Now I don't want to toot my own horn or make you think that I am ingenious. Nor do I want you to get the impression that I spend my days watching television. But it was indeed another commercial that saved the day.

Oh you've seen it. The stuff that can fix just about anything you break. You can hang by a hard hat suspended from a ceiling joist with it. I figured I could take a little bit of that liquid gold and glue the two mattresses together. The new mattress pad would stay in place and I would no longer feel as though I was falling. Great, huh? Sometimes I amaze myself with how smart I am. It's almost scary to realize that all that intelligence is securely wrapped up inside my little ol' head.

Now I just need to go watch one more commercial. You know, the one that tells you what product to use to get the dang sheets unstuck.

Chapter 17

Beware the Eyes of March

A couple of years back the first day of spring packed a wallop here in Texas. We had snow. A lot of it in some places. Now mind you, compared to many other places in our wonderful country, our winter was baby sized.

What's a few inches of snow when parts of the northeast got a few *feet* of the fluffy white stuff? In my opinion, we had just enough to entertain the kids and many adults, for that matter. But, it will be nice to store the mittens and scarves away and bring out the sandals and tee shirts. Yeah baby. I can feel the spring in my step already.

Quite frankly, spring is one of those seasons that just kind of happens. It comes in kind of quietly, as though it doesn't want to cause a fuss. The birds seem to sing a little louder in the morning. The sunrise seems to glow with the promise of a warmer, gentler day. And then all of a sudden you notice that people around you seem to have shed about 20 pounds of outer layers. I didn't think it was humanly possible for my husband to wear so many shirts at once and still be able to tuck them in his jeans but every winter he accomplishes this feat.

Better Late Than Never – Nansii Downer

And of course, as we all know, it is the time when people seem to get magically tanned before your very eyes. Bronzed skin replaces the pasty white winter look. Golden brown hairless legs are proudly displayed everywhere I go. It's amazing really. The sun has been out for maybe a few days, yet the folks around town look like they have been vacationing in the Bahamas for weeks.

This happens every year. Everyone's eyes are riveted to all of the tanned legs walking around. How do they do it? I noticed this a few years ago so, being blessed with having my own *Fashionista* in the family, I called her so that I might find out how this is accomplished.

It seems that scientists, bless their hearts, have developed ways to instantly tan you so that at the very first moment of crop pant season, you are ready to go. And it all comes, easy as pie, in a bottle or a tube.

I decided that it would be a good idea to try this stuff out, since I didn't want to be the only one out walking around looking so pale and sickly. Fitting in with the crowd is so important you know. So, off I go, to the neighborhood drug store to pick up a bottle of this wonderful potion. Now, like many of the "must have" items on the store shelves, this stuff is not cheap. Always trying to be the good steward, I pick up one that promises me a "glowing natural tan in just a few hours," for quite a bit less than the name brand that the *Fashionista* had suggested. She may know products and fashions, but I know how to save a buck.

After a good shave (remember, it's been winter time so the extra hair on the legs has been hidden by sweat pants); I squirt some of the gel in my hands and proceed to rub it on my legs. It is white, practically the same color as my legs, and it appears to disappear quickly and efficiently. It doesn't even really smell bad. I smile to myself just thinking about how awesome it is going to be in the morning when I put on my crop pants and sandals and no longer blind the neighbors when I walk out to get the mail.

The next morning as I made the coffee, I couldn't help but notice that my palms had kind of a glow in the dark look to them. They had a tinge of orange, like I had been eating Cheetos and not washed my hands properly. I washed them and dried them again, and then again, and to my utter surprise this dull orangy hue didn't go away.

I kept turning them over and over staring in amazement, having absolutely no idea why this was happening. Was I sick or something? Should I call the doctor and make an appointment? Was my liver shutting down??????? And then, like a bolt of lightning, it hit me. If my hands look like this, what in the world are my LEGS gonna look like?

I dashed for the bathroom and stood in front of the mirror intently staring at my orange legs. Where was the golden bronze tan that everybody else had?

The picture on the front of the bottle displayed the most wonderfully evenly tanned person I had ever seen. I wanted to look like HER, for heavens sake! Instead, I looked like a kindergartner had attempted to paint me and didn't understand the concept of staying in the lines. I looked like I had been haphazardly dipped in orange gelatin. My legs resembled a heavier version of my orange tabby cat.

What was I going to do?

The weather was supposed to be warm and sunny. People were expecting me to be ready for spring. For heaven's sake I had even had my toenails painted with a flower already.

There was no way around the fact that I was going to remain in this condition for a couple of weeks. I just couldn't let anyone see me like this. What would my friends think?

Would they pity me for this ghastly mistake or would they think to themselves that I must be really really ill and be polite and not say anything? I was secretly praying that a freak snowstorm would come so that everyone would be back to wearing parkas and mukluks. *But no.* As luck would have it, the weather was beautiful. Everywhere I went, in my blue jeans, people were showing off their tans and crop pants. I was an outcast among my own kind. I had no style, no glam. All I had was *orange legs*.

This year will be different. I heard about a place where they actually spray the tan right on you. Yeah. It's true. My girlfriend had it done. She came out of the stall, shiny bronze without so much of a stripe on her. Her legs had that even glow of being out in the sun continuously for weeks. I knew instantly that this was for me. No more magic potion from a bottle. I was going to go get that perfect tan. I called her up and she graciously explained the process to me.

I was doing great until she reached the part where you are naked in the stall as the person sprays the tan on you. I thought about this scenario and thought about it again. Was I willing to go to that length for a tan? Naked in a room with a person I didn't know? Naked in a room? Naked? At this stage in my life, nobody sees me naked on purpose. I just couldn't do it. I have no nerve. I have no chutzpah. But thank goodness I do have another coupon for the "Tan in a Bottle".

Better Late Than Never – Nansii Downer

Chapter 18

Spring is in the Air

With warmer weather finally arriving in North Texas it is time to open up the windows and breathe in the wonderful fragrance of blooming flowers. The Carolina jasmine that is hanging across our fence down the driveway mingles with the Star jasmine to create the most amazing sweet smell. The roses in my neighbors garden smell and look gorgeous. For me, there is nothing that quite compares to a freshly mowed lawn either. Life is good.

Growing up in a real family-friendly neighborhood brings back the memories of Easter egg hunts, baskets brimming with jelly beans, Peeps and of course a Helen Grace Chocolate Easter Egg. I get all goose pimply just thinking about those eggs. They were *huge*. Rich, creamy, melt in your mouth chocolate with an even creamier, dreamier walnut chocolate filling. These eggs were so big you had to slice pieces off with a butter knife. Mounds and mounds of chocolate-covered this and sugar-filled that. Life was soooo tasty.

Our neighborhood also gathered together to have the annual Easter Egg Hunt. We kids would wait for what seemed like hours as the parents hid all of those marvelously colored eggs around the bushes and trees on the street. Then, with our empty baskets ready, we would launch out on the wildest race to see who could find and claim the most eggs. Dashing here and there, grabbing eggs and shrieking with pure joy. **Life was breathless.**

Once I started my own family, I declared that I too, would keep these wonderful traditions alive. Each year, I would scour the candy aisles to get the best, most dazzling candies to surprise and amaze my children. I would spend hours in the kitchen, late at night, when the little darlings were asleep, hard boiling the eggs and then preparing them to be gently dipped in the vinegar and dye.

Watching...
    Watching...
        Watching...

...as they magically changed into the colors of the rainbow. To this day I love that smell. It triggers such wonderful memories of time gone by. Once the eggs dried I would place them ever so lovingly around the house and the yard knowing that my kids too, would dance with glee on this wonderful adventure of the hunt. **Life was exciting.**

Just like any other holiday, Easter only lasts so long. Within a couple of days, the "good" candy that was so lovingly placed in those adorable baskets is gone, and most of the green plastic basket grass has been cut off the beater bar of the vacuum. We have consumed more egg salad sandwiches than the FDA recommends and are beginning to look ahead to the next celebratory time.

But then something odd catches my attention. I can't quite place it. I follow the scent throughout the living room certain that something must have died somewhere within the walls of my home. There must be a dead animal up in the attic.

Life gets smelly.

As with any adventure or learning experience in life, it is important that we look to these moments and decide that we will become better, smarter people because of them. What is the sense of not taking every opportunity we are given and sharing those moments with the ones we love? Little life lessons I call them. The "something to write home about" stuff that makes us stronger and wiser. We can administer our wealth of knowledge to those younger ones, struggling to bring to their families the best holiday memories that money can buy. Sage advice from those who have been there, done that. Count the dang eggs BEFORE you hide them.

Life... just gets...

Better Late Than Never – Nansii Downer

Chapter 19

Hair Today, Gone Tomorrow

I am sure everyone has had a bad hair day from time to time. Some days there is simply not enough conditioner on the planet to tame this mop of mine. It is extremely curly and as unruly as a two year old having a fit at the candy counter. I am thinking that if I traced my family tree back a few hundred years or so, my hair DNA must have had a curse put on it. There is no other reason that I can think of. After all, you know me... I *am* a nice person.

In my younger years, and of course youth gives me no excuse for bad behavior, I could hardly hide my disdain for people who grew hair, in my opinion, where hair really shouldn't be.

There I was standing in line patiently at the grocery store, making idle conversation with the person behind me, when all of a sudden my eyes would be riveted on these little wisps of hair. I'm not talking about a hair or two being out of place here either. Oh, no, no, no, my friends. I am referring to the moment when they turn their head and the light catches these 4 inch hairs growing from their earlobes or chins. I had to cover my child's eyes for fear that they would have been terrified at the sight of that. I was almost speechless, and the conversation ended with me mumbling something about them having a good day and vowing that this would *never* happen to me.

My "moment in the sun" came on a beautiful spring day while at the ballpark with the family. We were all kicking back enjoying the game, while feasting on nachos and soda. The grandkids were having a great time and my daughter and I, sitting side by side, were busy catching up on the news of work and family. All of a sudden, mid bite mind you, she stares at me with her mouth gaping open and says,

"Mother!!! My gosh, what is on your chin?"

My first constructive thought was that I must have a smidgen of melted cheese on my chin from the nachos. Makes sense right????? I gently dab at my chin with the napkin and then turn to her and say, "There. Did I get it?"

Before I can finish wiping my face she has turned and is frantically going through her purse desperately seeking something and all the while mumbling to herself about this shameful situation. The next thing I know she has whipped out a pair of tweezers and has grabbed ahold of my chin as she

"tsk, tsk, tsks" me.

Better Late Than Never – Nansii Downer

Then she begins to pluck, pluck, pluck me!!!!

Now, it is not that I am an overly private kind of person, but hey, plucking my chin at the ballpark is not something that I would consider as a day at the spa. She even calls my husband and son-in-law over to take a gander at the atrocity of the situation. Well, let me tell you, I made a firm decision to never let this happen again. How, or better yet, when, did I become the person from the grocery store line? How does a nice person like me, turn into hairy monstrosity overnight? I must get a handle on this whole thing and NOW.

Wearing glasses and trying to see myself in a mirror has become quite a challenge these last few years. As I stood at the bathroom sink, poised and ready with tweezers in hand, I realized that with the bifocals in my lenses, my chin area became just a blur of flesh colored material. I couldn't see the hair much less try to grab them with the tip of these itsy bitsy tweezers.

So I called in my husband for reinforcement. He put on his reading glasses thinking that it would give him just the right view and clarity. Nope. He couldn't see what he was doing either. Being an Internet surfer from way back, he decides that we can get all the direction we needed from the web and proceeds to look up "hair removal". Lots of wonderful products pop up and we read all about them. We make our decision and off we go to the store to buy wax strips. "This should get the job done," he says smiling.

Sitting in a chair with my head tilted back, I watch with amazement, as my loving husband rubs the wax strips in his palms to get them good and soft and ready to do their job. He gently peels the paper off and then applies them to my chin massaging them so they will get "all of the hair". No stragglers left on this pretty face.

>He straightens up,
>>rubs his hands together,
>>>gives his knuckles a good crack
>>>>…and says, "Ready"?

Before I can suck in a breath he yanks as hard as he can, practically ripping me out of the chair. **Good night Agnes!** Are these things made of crazy glue? I feel like the bottom portion of my face has been permanently removed. I am waiting for the blood flow to start.

Do people really *do* this all the time?

My husband, bless his heart, has now made it his mission to keep all those nasty hairs from building up on my pretty little face. At the drop of a hat, or a stray ray of sunshine, he will lovingly offer to groom me.

Better Late Than Never – Nansii Downer

My, my, I am one lucky gal, huh? He doesn't even complain about doing it. Nope, not at all. He sets to his work almost joyfully. What's that? Maybe too joyfully? You don't really think, do you... he is enjoying this far too much?????

Well I never...
                ever...
                              would have thought of that.

You don't think that is why I just happened to notice a little stray ear hair that I will need to take care of for him, do you? Hell hath no fury like a woman with a spare wax strip.

Better Late Than Never – Nansii Downer

Chapter 20

Does this Suit Suit Me?

With my family reunion lurking in the not too distant future, it is time to once again gather my senses and realize that I must go out and do the unthinkable. You know, the thing that makes women shiver to their very bones. It makes grown men who have to go with them quake in fear of saying the wrong thing. Yep. You know it. It is time to go and get a new bathing suit.

I am not sure how other states in the union introduce their "seasonal" wear? But here in the great state of Texas, the department stores pack up everything even remotely considered warm, and stock the aisles with bathing suits while the snow is still on the ground. I am sure that their marketing people feel that we shoppers need this little reminder of brighter sunnier days in our future, right? Or could it be that they have taken a very close look at us and realized that we gotta start *now* if we think for even one moment that we are going to fit into one of the latest and greatest swimsuits.

My philosophy is to pick a time during the day when most other female shoppers are NOT going to be shopping. There is just something about trying on bathing suits in front of lesser women that sets my teeth on edge. A size 4 has absolutely no business being in the same dressing room area as a size 12. They need to respect my space because, trust me, I need more than they do in that fitting room area. I am still pulling and tucking while they are out in the center of the fitting room prancing around and twirlin' in front of the full length mirror while I am cowered on the floor of the fitting room with one leg stuck inside the suit that I swear should have fit, and didn't.

Last year, I tried on one that was supposed to give me the look that I wanted.

Thin.
Vibrant.
Sexy.

Did I say thin???? I refer to this suit as the Bluffakini. It comes in cute patterns and prints and its claim to fame is that it can hold anything on anyone "in".

Think about this, girls. A bikini that will HOLD you in. "In where?" was my first thought. I have tried unsuccessfully to hold "this" in, so how in the world can a bikini do it? But, never one to be doubtful, because after all, we all know that advertisers would never make a false claim, I pick one up and head for the dressing room. Once I get over the shock of seeing myself nearly nude, I begin the process of trying on my

Better Late Than Never – Nansii Downer

Bluffakini. It takes a good 15 minutes to tuck everything in and I am bent over trying to catch my breath because I feel like I have just climbed a flight of stairs. Stuffing and shoving and hiding is hard work! With reddened cheeks from all of the exertion, I glance in the mirror. Hmm. Not bad. The Bluffakini has successfully trimmed and thinned me. I can't breathe mind you, but it hadn't advertised anything about breathing.

Here is the only flaw that I could see, and trust me I SAW this one. The Bluffakini made my backside UN-teeny. The front view looked all nice and trim while the view from the side resembled a **rising dough ball.** Like at any moment I was going to have a pressure build up and explode. One big bounce while on the boat could send me skyward like an overfilled balloon that someone released. I must admit, in my naivete I wasn't sure where all of the tucking and shoving stuff was going to end up, but it shouldn't have ended up THERE for heavens sake. Shouldn't the view from any given angle been one of a sleek athlete? Even with my wonder tan, **I looked like a freshly baked pretzel.**

So here we are. Knowing full well that this year will be no different, that the times and size, they ain't a changin', I am once more in search of the perfect bathing suit for family reunion. Will it be within my grasp this year or as in years past, will it leave me just... gasping for air.

Better Late Than Never – Nansii Downer

Chapter 21

What Goes Around Goes to Round

Let's face it. Dieting has been around, well.... since Adam and Eve. I have even heard a rumor that the Devil told her that the apple was less fattening than the figs so that might have been why she ate it so readily. Mind you, had he mentioned the part about painful childbirth she might have reconsidered, but you know what they say about hindsight. Having given birth a few times myself, I would have opted for the calories and a longer walk around the garden.

Speaking of round , why is it that "round" foods are not on most dieters' lists? Come on now, follow me here, OK? Let's start with a donut. The operative word being "A" donut. Personally, I have never been served a donut that I turned up my nose at and just ate it to be polite.

Let's face it. Coffee and donuts have been a staple at most church fellowship events and even have found their way into business meetings. I have often times delivered a dozen of these delectables for the opportunity to meet a new business person and of course just *had* to sit and enjoy one with them. Haven't you? And why on earth do 2 donuts always taste better than just 1? Or how about the meet and greet cookie brigade? I am the first one signed up to go and bring cookies to a new person in the neighborhood. There is such a sweet reward when you do this. Take a few, eat a few is my motto.

Let's take just a moment and explore some of the "roundies" that *don't* get a bad wrap. A head of broccoli or cauliflower for example; they are round when you buy them. But when you serve them, they are pulled apart and disguised as "florets". No more round, no more calories.

Oranges. Peel 'em, break 'em apart and voila... they become wedges. No more round. Grapes are another example of the injustice. They are round AND they come in bunches but because you have to pull them off the stem to enjoy them, that act would be considered exercise, hence no calories. Do I detect a pattern here?

Over the years the good folks that bring you all the delicious round foods, have tried to be shape changers. A donut isn't really a round food if you have it in a bar form. Like a lemon filled bar or an éclair. These are rectangles. And what about the cheesy, gooey pizza that no longer is round but is a deep dish square. This should be OK too, right? I once witnessed the guy at the ice cream counter deliver to me a "cube"-shaped ice cream cone, because after all round things don't have corners, so you guessed it... calories should have disappeared, don't you think?

Now, I have never claimed to be a Rocket Scientist or anything but hey, it seems to me that something could be done about this injustice. It is almost politically incorrect to be a round food anymore. Someone should take up the cause and fight for what is right. I am tired of the clandestine Round Food Eaters Anonymous meetings, aren't you? The burying of the round foods at the bottom of the grocery basket so that no one knows what you are buying is shameful really. Round foods have feelings too ya know!!! They must come together and fight for the right to be who they are. No longer should they stay hidden in pantries across the world.

                              Tortillas,
                    potato chips,
            donuts,
       cookies,
   bagels,

It is time to unite!

Just not on my waistline, OK?

Better Late Than Never – Nansii Downer

Chapter 22

The Hunched Back of Noted Dame

Right up front I want to admit that *I am not* a girly girl. I do not "shop until I drop", nor do I make it my life's quest to have an "ensemble", much to the *Fashionista's* chagrin I must say, but hey, I am over 21 now and can make up my own mind where my fashion loyalties will be.

I don't need to read every magazine about the colors of the season, what's hot and what's not, or when it's acceptable to wear white pants in public. I mean, come on now, we ALL know the rules concerning the proper etiquette where white pants are concerned, right? Try as I may to conform, the little rebel comes out in me and I always find a reason to wear my white pants *before* Memorial Day. *Mu-hahaha!!!!!*

Another thing I have never really taken a shine to is changing purses to go with that oh-so-perfect ensemble. I am a woman of many needs, most of which I carry in my purse. I have my little lipstick bag, just in the *off chance* I decide to actually wear the stuff. There is the semi small bottle of hand lotion, and coupons, just in case I stop at the store. I carry a butter knife for all those times that I might have to cut a sandwich in pieces for the little ones. Those *"little ones"* now have little ones of their own. Kleenex, handi-wipes, mints. You name it. If you need it, I probably can find it in the bottom of my purse. I carry the current year's calendar booklet as well as last year's. You never know when someone might need to know what you did last year. The measuring tape with the itty-bitty flashlight came in real handy when I dropped my cell phone in my purse and couldn't find it. A good purse, with all of the basics, is what a woman of my stature needs. She also needs a good chiropractor.

I recently saw a photo of myself in a group of smiling friends. We girls had been out to dinner or some other fun thing and someone in the crowd snapped a picture. I looked as though I was trying to walk in the Ghost Town's Haunted Shack at Knott's Berry Farm.

Why in the world was I *leaning to the left* so much?

All my friends were standing up straight and tall and I appeared to need a really quick refresher course on good posture. And then I looked a little closer. What in the world were all the little sparkling dots at my waist? It was the bling from the strap of my purse twinkling in the flash of the camera. All of those essentials in my purse were actually causing me to look like a drunken sailor on a Saturday night.

That night when I got home I did the old twist and turn in the bathroom mirror. I turned from side to side over and over again to try and get a view of the enormous muscle in my shoulder from totin' around this suitcase. Hot dang man, I looked like a whiter version of the Incredible Hulk from the left. Believe it or not, I really thought about getting on the scale and weighing myself with the baggage and without. When did my purse become a weight lifting event for the Olympics? I should be getting a gold medal for carrying this thing around everyday.

So I decided that it was time to clean out the old purse. I sat at the dining room table and my husband brought me the kitchen trash can so that I could do the "toss and go". I figured it would probably take me just a few minutes to clear out some of the necessary things that might be the cause of the chunkiness of the purse.

You know, the *actual* non-essentials; receipts for things that I couldn't wear again if my life depended on it, gum wrappers from all those times that there wasn't a trash can close by, pens that had run out of ink years ago, little scraps of paper that must have had important notes on them at some point, but were now no more than smudges of ink.

There. I had done it.

I had cleaned out my purse. All that was left in the wake of this cleaning would be the important things.

Better Late Than Never – Nansii Downer

The must-haves.
> The things that come in handy in a pinch.
>> The things that *still weigh a ton*.

I decided that a clean light purse was not in my near future, so yes, you know it, I have learned to carry it on the right side, and soon I will be a balanced woman again!

Chapter 23

Come on Baby Light My Fire

Men. Ya gotta love 'em, right? Even when they do some of the most hair-brained things. Not only do they attempt to DO these things, they then get together and *brag* to each other about their latest and greatest accomplishments with no earthly idea how the *really smart ones*, we women, are viewing them.

Case in point: Starting a fire. Oh not just any fire, but one that is *in the house*, in the fireplace. Or at least that is where it should be. Let me take you back to a cool night in November. We had cooked and eaten the wonderful Thanksgiving feast that I have lovingly slaved over all day. All in about 30 minutes after sitting down, I must add.

I am in the kitchen loading the dishwasher. My dear husband decides that he is going to start a fire. Okay, I know what you are thinking,

"What could possibly be wrong with that?"

Oh friends!!!! A fire starter he is not. It just doesn't seem to come naturally to him. Some people know exactly how to bunch the paper up nice and tight so that you have good kindling. I don't think marrying an Eagle Scout is a necessity, but where fires are concerned, let's just say *being prepared* would come in handy.

After several attempts to get the kindling to catch, my husband got a wee bit frustrated. What do husbands do in a case like this? They holler for their wives to come and give them a hand, of course. Well, I only made it to Brownies in my scouting life, so my fire starting experience is also limited. As a matter of fact, I normally use those logs that just kind of light magically by themselves. Rolling up newspaper is just so dad gummed messy too. Black ink all over your hands... well that's a different story.

Anyway, after a few lights, relights and words that a lady won't mention, he gives up. I offer to go to the store and buy a "log" but with a gleam in his eye, he says that won't be necessary. He knows exactly how to get it started. On goes the coat and out to the garage he goes. He returns in a few minutes and begins the process of scrunching up newspaper all over again. Full of new confidence that my wonderful husband will soon have a toasty fire going I wander back to the kitchen to resume my task.

In my mind I am thinking how nice it will be to sit down by the fire with our feet on the coffee table relaxing and just having a nice quite evening when, "WHOOOOOSH!!!!"

Out of the corner of my eye I see something go shooting into the dining room. I grab the kitchen towel (it's never a good idea to drip water on the clean floor, just ask Martha) and make a dash for the dining room. There on the floor is a singed and smelly version of my husband, smoke still floating around him. He is carefully wiping his now almost-gone eyebrows with a sheepish look on his face. His sweater, the new one I had just gotten him, is the most awful pukey brown color.

Honest to goodness, I just stood there. I didn't even know what to say. I really didn't even know how he got over there. And then it hit me. I slowly turned and looked towards the fireplace. A huge roaring fire was crackling away.

"Pretty cool huh?" is all he said.

You see, lighting the fire the old fashioned way was just taking too long. So? Why not speed things up a bit. And what better way to get a fire going than to use the white gas that you have stored in the garage for all of those family camping trips?

Duh! Why didn't *I* think of that??? I'll tell you why. Because *SANE* people don't use white gas to start a fire in a fireplace, that's why!!! It seems that in his rush to get the fire started, he got heavy handed with the gas. It kept putting the matches out. Sooooooo, when he finally got it to light, the gas fumes formed a ball of flame and shot him across the room, thus making that whooshing sound.

Better Late Than Never – Nansii Downer

Fast forward to Sunday morning at church. Everyone meeting and greeting each other. Talking about the holiday weekend, football, big turkey dinners. The normal stuff.

Then I noticed all the men-folk gathered around my husband listening to him like he was offering up some well meaning advice. All of a sudden, they all start high fiving him and patting him on the back, shaking their heads and making that grunting sound that made television history. He has retold them the story of the white gas!!!! And he is now their hero. They marvel at him. The do a little victory dance in the parking lot. They gather him into their fold.

He is now one of them!

Chapter 24

Cutting Off my Knows to Spite My Weight

Looking at labels on food products has become my reading of choice lately. It seems that there is just no getting around it.

    Calories,
        fat grams,
            sodium.

Who would have ever guessed that a simple peanut butter and jelly sandwich would need a calculator and a note pad lying nearby?

    Journal entries,
        adding this
            and replacing with that.

The thrill of victory when the numbers balance at the end of the day. The groans of agony when they don't. I don't get this riled up when the checkbook doesn't balance. But let my intake be greater than my recommended allotment and well… it can wear a girl out.

Better Late Than Never – Nansii Downer

Watching my weight has almost become a new pastime for my husband and me. It is almost like a hobby that we share together. Who knew something so seemingly mundane as a diet, could bring us even closer together? We share intimate conversations daily now.

You know... like, "Wow honey, did ya notice the fat grams in that thing?"

Or, "How can anything as light and fluffy as popcorn possibly have that many calories!"

We spend lazy afternoons together, slowly strolling down the aisles of the grocery store, side by side, gazing lovingly at the ingredient labels. Who would have guessed that the prime of our lives would have come to this?

You see, I am married to *the informer*. If you need to know anything about anything, he either knows it, or by gosh he can find out. He has the memory of an elephant in full regalia when it comes to my calorie and water intake for the day. He knows exactly how many glasses I should consume and he's not afraid to share that information. It's almost like he has this little calculator inside his head and pushes the memory button whenever I am in the kitchen. "You gettin' some water while you're there girlfriend?" he will joyfully holler from another room. In fact, just to spite him, I *will* pour myself a full glass of water and drink it down. *So there.* Take that mister. You're not gonna tell *ME* what to do. After all, I do know what's best.

Since math has never been my strong suit, I guess it is pretty convenient to have a mobile calculator at my fingertips. He can tally the score in his head for anything on the menu at a fast food restaurant long before I have made up my mind as to what I am even going to have. Now mind you, he never ever makes a recommendation of one "delicious" versus more "nutritious". While I am deciding, he just wants to have the information on hand in the off chance that I might inquire. Like I didn't *know* that un-sweet tea is better for me than sweet tea. Come on, I am a Texan now. We drink sweet tea, by gum. Or that a chocolate milkshake probably will count for ALL of my intake for the day. Well, duhhhh!!! BUT... that milkshake would taste so good on a hot Texas day, right? I can make up for the extra intake numbers later, right? Like tomorrow? Or maybe next week?

It's a shame the ole diet thing doesn't really work that way.
Eat it today, wear it tomorrow.
Cookies at night, bring bigger shadows by day.

I am not quite sure what a good metabolism is, but I sure

didn't inherit one from my family. I don't know if I can *buy* a good metabolism but I am willing to have a garage sale to finance it.

Hey, wait a minute. What really goes well with a garage sale?????? Donuts and coffee in the morning while you set everything up and of course pizza at night since you are too tired to cook.

Who's with me????

Chapter 25

The Shedding

After a long day at work it is always a joy to come home. My husband and I start dinner and mull over our day. What we did, where we went. Normal conversations between normal people. Sometimes we even take a cup of coffee and go and sit on the porch for awhile. We watch the kids play in the yard across the street.

Lazy conversations… Idle chit-chat… Safe.

Secretive… Afraid…VERY AFRAID.

Neither of us wants to bring up the subject of the evil that lurks within our home.

It happens almost every morning. In normal homes. In quiet neighborhoods around the world. Folks starting their day, getting ready for work. Taking a nice hot shower. Picture it.

You turn on the faucet, wait for the water to get just the right temperature and step in drawing the shower curtain closed.

You look up at the shower head as the water gently cascades over your face and then it starts, the haunting, screeching violin... **REEE REEE REEE REEE.**

You feel it before you actually see it. But it's there. In the water. Coiling and snaking its way around your toes. Pulling you towards the drain where it will surely drag you to your death. At my house... we call this

"THE SHEDDING".

Strands of long natural curly hair hiding in the deepest recesses of the drain. Waiting, waiting, waiting for their next victim to step into the shower.

And then there's the bathroom sink. You wash your hands there, brush your teeth there. What could be safer? But every so often the water starts draining a little slower so you take the stopper out and peer down into the pipe thinking that maybe the kids have stuck something down there. Finally, you get a wire hanger and stick it down digging around to get a grip on the culprit. And what do you pull out? This giant ball of tangled hair that resembles a very small rodent.

It is... **"The Mouse"!**

Better Late Than Never – Nansii Downer

There isn't a plumber in the world that doesn't quake in his boots when he gets a call from a frantic homeowner asking for help to unclog a drain. I have seen with my very own eyes what comes out of there. These guys earn every penny.

At times it seems like I am a character actor from the Star Trek series. You remember the one I am talking about, don't you? The story of the Tribbles? The cute little balls of hair that suddenly started multiplying and eventually filling the entire ship? Or, it could be a scene from Gremlins. They were never supposed to get wet either. Maybe I have Gremlin DNA or something. I have not quite figured it out, but it certainly seems that no matter where I go or what I am doing I leave my signature shedding in my wake.

I was so depressed about this. Would I pass this terrible trait on to my unsuspecting children? Would they too, have people come up behind then and gently pluck the stray hairs off the back of their shirt? Would they carry the dreaded label of a shedder and become an outcast in society? Would they be taken off of the "A" list and not be invited to the company parties because... **well you know**... it could be catching. This was horrible. How was I ever going to survive this terrible fate that had been dealt to me?

And then it happened. A friend came out of the "shedding" closet and confessed that she too, was a shedder.

Better Late Than Never – Nansii Downer

I was stunned. Shocked. Speechless.

But secretly, quite frankly, I was overjoyed. If there were 2 of us, then maybe there were 3 of us. Could there be another shedder who needed a friend? A confidant? Someone who would understand that shedders should not be the scourge of the drainpipes? We could have meetings. Write books. Share our shedding stories. We could go worldwide with this. I could see it in my mind. Shedders from every walk of life, banding together and walking arm in arm demanding the respect that we deserved, never more to be taunted and humiliated by those who seemed to be able to keep their hair on their scalp. Or, we could just simply pluck the hair off of each other's back when no one else was looking, nod at each other and just know that we belonged to a secret elite group. Yeah. Maybe keeping it to ourselves is the best idea yet.

Chapter 26

The Heat is On

I am proud to announce that I am courageously making my way through the 50's. Oh, it has been somewhat of a challenge, but not nearly as bad as I thought. I have many friends who are older than I, so as long as I hang around them, I look and feel great. I remember when I used to kind of snicker at the "blue hairs" who would proudly announce their age and claim that they were "not getting older, they were getting better". Yeah right, I thought. But now, I chime that sentiment louder than anyone. **50 is indeed the new 35!!!!**

I had heard and paid close attention to, the prattling of my older friends as they seemed to go on and on about the "changes" that occurred once you crossed over into "never never land". Things like "You never see as clearly anymore", or "Your hair color will never be that shade of brown again". I dreaded the experience that I was sure that I would face.

The shape changing.
Things that hang low, where they shouldn't.
Creases in areas that seem to be permanent indentations.
Crow's feet, laugh lines, a 5 o'clock shadow.

For mercy's sake! These were all subtly coming

my way, sneaking up on this young at heart, perky, bubbly me, with a sadistic desire to bring the "signs of time" to my chin... and thighs... and my beautiful brown hair.

Although I haven't really noticed a lot of "changes" in my body recently, I am sure that they are lurking out there somewhere waiting to pounce on me when I least expect it. **Changes are good**, I have reminded myself. As long as I am in full awareness as to what the changes are and exactly when they might show up. It's not that I can't roll with the punches or anything because I can. I can readily adjust to most new and different things with a smile on my face. It's just, well, I have heard the horror stories of the so called changes we women go through and to be quite honest with you...

...most of them scare me to death.

Things that hang down where they shouldn't hang down, freaky squeaky noises from places a lady wouldn't discuss much less admit that those noises belonged to her and a strange urge to put doilies out. **My gosh will this happen to me????**

Back in my younger days, I could get around pretty good. I could exercise, go for a walk, get in and out of my car even, and not break a sweat. Heck, we never even admitted that we sweated. We glistened!!! Little diamond shaped beads of sweat droplets glistening in the mirror as we watched ourselves workout with our gym sisters. **Bending, stretching, stair stepping. We did it all.**

And we did it to the beat of music blasting all around us. We wore matching outfits with little leggings and looked, oh so cute, working out side by side. Nowadays, I need a full sized bath towel at my fingertips before I attempt to tie my own shoes. Slipping into something comfortable has become a quest to find the least amount of buttons, laces and strings to wrestle with. Give me the simple pleasures.

In all of the many conversations I have had about this growing older thing, no one took the time to tell me that I would eventually need to buy stock in a liniment company. *Oh my gosh!!!* When in the world did the simple process of rolling out of bed in the morning become the event from hell? A peaceful night's sleep and then **WHAM!!** Every joint pops, my knees crack and the pain in my back feels like I was joyriding in a car without shocks for the past several hours. Where was this phenom on the list of notes from the "over the hill gang"? Was anyone going to bother to tell me or was this the big surprise that I needed to experience all on my own? Either way, there is just no preparing for this. None, zip, nada!!

Better Late Than Never – Nansii Downer

My husband and I respect this new avenue in our lives. We have embraced it and learned to cope with it to the best of our ability. What choice do we have? After all, doesn't that license say something about for better or for worse? As in any good relationship you just learn to adjust. We give each other a little extra space as we move about... just in case one of us keels over from the pain of walking. We hold hands when we are out in public... in case one of us loses our balance. And we have efficiently learned how to apply liniment to each other's achy-breaky backs.

Chapter 27

Whistle Stop

Growing up in Southern California meant beautiful sunny days, warm, but not too hot temps, Disneyland fireworks on balmy summer nights and of course... **the Helm's man**. Just reminiscing about his visits gives me goose bumps. He was a giant among men. He knew how to work a crowd. He was a network marketing genius. He was in a class all his own. And it all started when we heard the **toot-toot** of his little whistle.

It didn't really matter to any of us what time of the day he showed up. It seemed as though entire neighborhoods stopped what they were doing at the earliest detection of that whistle. It could be early in the morning or late in the afternoon. It mattered not, as long as he made his way to our street.

Please, please, please, let this be the day when it was our turn for him to drive through our neighborhood. Every single mother from every single home seemed to appear almost magically, looking like June Cleaver in her pearls and apron, walking briskly out of her house to make her way to his truck. It was poetry in motion.

Better Late Than Never – Nansii Downer

He would cruise ever so slowly down the street and find just the right midway point and then ever soooo slowly apply his brakes and roll to a gentle stop. The driver's side door would open and out he would step. He was radiant in his white pants and white shirt. He seemed to almost glow. To all of us he was angelic. He would smile and welcome us and then... **and then... and then...** He would open the back doors of his early '60's beige suburban and the most heavenly smell would waft through the air and the anticipation would begin.

The inside of the truck consisted of many wooden drawers. Each one was pulled out with great love and care to reveal the most delicious donuts and breads you could imagine.

Jelly filled,
    Chocolate covered sprinkles,
Eclairs filled to the max with scrumptious vanilla custard.

The drawers just seemed to go on forever as he would pull them out one at a time.

...Rows and rows and rows of **warm, gooey, sugar coated, jelly filled circles of heaven,** all just waiting to be bought and wrapped in that little special sized piece of waxed paper, and handed over to a ready recipient.

Better Late Than Never – Nansii Downer

As our good mothers carefully picked out their loaves of bread, we kids would sit on the curb and savor our donuts. We didn't think about the calories or the quantity of sugar as it made a little mustache on our lips. We didn't even know where this guy came from or if his product followed the FDA guidelines. We just knew that every once in a while we would hear the toot-toot of a whistle off in the distance, grab our Moms and make a mad dash for that old beige truck.

Life was simple. Life was good.
Life was made sweeter because of the Helm's man!

Better Late Than Never – Nansii Downer

Chapter 28

A Little Dab Will Do Ya

There are many beauty products on the market today. We have scientifically come up with a way to solve every personal hygiene problem known to man. Or animal for that matter. If it smells bad we have a myriad of products just waiting on our store shelves to make those around us let go of their noses. Shampoos, deodorants, toiletries galore. Waiting, just waiting for the right consumer to pluck them off of the shelf and take them home. From the 'frugal' to the 'more-money-than-they-know-what-to-do-with' crowd, we have it all. Neatly packaged. Conveniently located at a store near you.

Progress, baby. That's what I call progress.

Now, I really don't want to show my age here, but I swear to you, I remember a time in the not so distant past, when you would apply hair products so you would lose that fly-away look. Or the "my gosh, it must be humid outside" frizz. And we had the perfect fix for that youngin' that had a titch of a cowlick. You know the one. When spit wouldn't hold it down, you pulled out the big gun. Hair gel number 8!!

We seem to have evolved into a new socially acceptable era. I must have slept in the day it was announced, but whose idea was it that it is now an acceptable practice to have your hair mussed purposely and be considered quite the fashion statement?

Oh yes, I have contacted the *Fashionista* on this and she immediately went into the vapors and had to have the smelling salts brought to her. She has never seen anything like this "in all her born days". Why it is just shameful I tell you.

Have you people ever SEEN my hair in the morning???

My goodness it looks as though I have stuck my finger into a light socket. A really *big* light socket at that. I have spent countless hours in front of the bathroom mirror trying to get it under control and now it's been decided that the bed head look is *in*?

Are you people crazy???

I have decided that I shall rebel. That's right, I said rebel. I am going to march to a different drummer. I am not, I repeat NOT, going to give in to my peers. I shall continue to take my time each and every morning armed with all of those wonderful products that my fellow man has spent so much time developing for me.

    I will rub it in,
        Spray it on,
            Comb it through,
                Pat it down,
                    Mousse it out,

until I have reached the level of "coiffed-ness" that you all have come to know and love. If you see me in a crowd, I will be the one standing tall and proud with hair that neither moves in the wind or is affected by a sudden downpour. Yep, that right!! You got it. I am a rebel. Not one single hair out of place. Poised and ready to face the day and its challenges. And off to work to earn more money for them dad-gum products. Progress baby, progress.

Better Late Than Never – Nansii Downer

Chapter 29

Bad Moon Rising

Oh, yes. It has been another great weekend. Going from here to there. Seeing all of the wonderful sights that any great city has to offer. It is pretty much the same no matter what part of the country you travel to. People and places begin to look about the same. Well, at least in the city that is. Go ahead. I dare you. Take a walk with your beloved on your arm and stroll down the streets of any metropolitan city.

You'll see it.

You will be standing, minding your own business and someone will walk by. Or maybe sitting at a quaint little table outside a coffee house, enjoying a frappe and then you spot it. Colorful underwear riding high and pants riding low.

What is the fascination of walking around with your britches hangin' out? Do you not know that your mother spent a lot of money on belts for this very reason???? This is not something that girls do, mind you. Oh, no. This is reserved for the guys. The pants or shorts that they have on hang down to the middle of their knees, and their brightly colored underwear sticks out by about 4 inches. I gotta ask... why???? Is this like some kind of a rite of passage for young men? Showin' your chonies to the world? Is there like some big testosterone rush you get from people staring at you? I admit it. I just don't get it at all.

And then there is the walking. Or the attempting to walk, I should say. Stumbling around trying to look so cool as they try to keep their balance so they won't fall over. And at the same time, they appear to be trying to hold up their pants with their free hand. That is what they are trying to do, isn't it??? It is just not natural to walk like that. It produces almost a limp for heavens' sake. Mark my words, young man, you are going to need a chiropractor one of these days!!!

Save yourself while you are still young!!!

Of late, I have seen billboards requesting that you no longer share this fad with the rest of us. There have even been mayoral campaigns that have emerged on this very issue. Proclamations of change. Songs sung on television promoting pulling up those pants!!! Oh, I know, we should allow you to do your own thing, much like we did in our hey days. But come on now. Show us older more genteel folk some much deserved mercy and grace here. The top of your tighty-whiteys is not something that I have personally lived this long to see. And yes, I indeed have lived a good long time. And I do know fashion. Well at least I have a *Fashionista* in the family who herself swears that this practice is just well, "Not Nice".

At least the young fashion minded girls don't do this. Oh, no. They are much too respectable to go walking around town with their undergarments hanging over the top of their pants. No way. They prefer the more subtle look. You know, like they **don't even have any on!!!** No unsightly panty lines for them. They have chosen to wear a piece of elastic for their underwear. Yep. You heard me right. A *thin* piece of elastic. When they walk by, you don't even notice it. But, here is the catch. It shows, and brother how it shows, when they happen to bend over right in front of you to reach for something that they probably didn't need or want in the first place. The shirt rises up... the top of the pants s t r e t c h down and voila, elastic so thin that it has to leave chaffing.

This has got to be painful.

I have never really been inclined to wear things of this sort, even in my younger thinner days. Oh they have been around for many years, but they have never intrigued me. Why would a young woman purposely put something on that is going to give 'em a rash?? In my day, we were stepping out of the box when we got bikini underwear. Now there's daring!!! Or, and I probably shouldn't admit this... but I really was quite the rebel and trendsetter. Oh yeah!!! Remember those cute little undies that had the days of the week embroidered on them??? Well... I would wear the red 'Saturday' ones on other days. Like Sunday, when we went to church. Yep. I was bold. Yep. I was livin' on the edge. And all the while, it was my little secret. I didn't share my little fashion secret with the whole world. Maybe you all shouldn't either. Some things are better kept *under wraps*.

www.ingramcontent.com/pod-product-compliance
Lightning Source LLC
Chambersburg PA
CBHW071705040426
42446CB00011B/1928